American Moments

ABDO
& Daughters

BILL OF RIGHTS

By Sheila Rivera

VISIT US AT
WWW.ABDOPUB.COM

Published by ABDO Publishing Company, 4940 Viking Drive, Suite 622, Edina, Minnesota 55435. Copyright ©2004 by Abdo Consulting Group, Inc. International copyrights reserved in all countries. No part of this book may be reproduced in any form without written permission from the publisher.

Printed in the United States.

Edited by: Cory Gunderson
Contributing Editors: Jessica A. Klein
Cover Design: Mighty Media
Interior Production and Design: Terry Dunham Incorporated
Photos: Corbis, Library of Congress

Library of Congress Cataloging-in-Publication Data

Rivera, Sheila, 1970-
    The Bill of Rights / Sheila Rivera.
        p. cm. -- (American moments)
    Summary: Explores the rights guaranteed by the first ten amendments to the Constitution, why that Bill of Rights was considered necessary, and how it formed the basis of similar documents in the United States and abroad.
    Includes bibliographical references and index.
    Contents: The struggle for human rights -- Magna Carta and the English Bill of rights -- Virginia Declaration of Rights -- French Declaration of Rights of Man and the Citizen -- United States Bill of Rights -- Universal human rights.
    ISBN 1-59197-279-5
    1. United States. Constitution. 1st-10th Amendments--Juvenile literature. [1. United States. Constitution. 1st-10th Amendments. 2. Constitutional amendments--United States. 3. Civil rights.] I. Title. II. Series.

KF4750.R58 2003
342.73'085--dc21
                                                                    2003052280

CONTENTS

THE STRUGGLE FOR HUMAN RIGHTS

When we think of rights, we often think of the rights that governments grant their citizens. These are called civil rights. They may include the right to vote, freedom of speech, and religious freedom. These are just a few of the civil rights granted to U.S. citizens. The United States also grants its citizens the right to a fair trial, freedom of the press, and freedom from unlawful searches.

There are other kinds of rights, too. Some of them are extended to people of all nations. These rights are called human rights. Some human rights are the right to life and liberty, freedom of thought and expression, and equality before the law. Human rights are the basics of natural law.

The idea of natural law began in Greece. The Greeks thought that there were certain laws that were basic and fundamental to human nature. These laws are not taught. Instead, they are discovered through reason. They include morals, or knowing what is right and fair, knowing right from wrong, and having good character. Natural law is the basis for most civil rights.

The first ten amendments to the U.S. Constitution are called the Bill of Rights. The First Amendment guarantees U.S. citizens freedom of speech, freedom of expression, and the right to gather peacefully. When people stage demonstrations, they are exercising their First Amendment rights.

Pages from the official program of the Woman Suffrage Procession from 1913. Thousands of women marched in The Woman Suffrage Parade of 1913 to protest laws that prevented them from voting. These women were called suffragists.

Throughout history, people have negotiated and sometimes even fought with their governments to gain certain civil rights. People have had to fight to keep their rights when threatened with losing them. Governments have not always offered equal rights to all people. Civil rights are not always the same from one country to the next.

In the early days of the United States, men and women did not have the same rights. In fact, women were not allowed to vote in this country until 1920. Before then, men made all government decisions.

When slaves were brought to the United States from Africa, they did not have the same rights as European settlers. Slaves were denied many basic rights. They were considered the property of their owners. They were forced to live and work in places determined by their owners. They were not allowed to speak their native languages. Slaves were not allowed to vote either.

European settlers took away the rights of the Native Americans, too. Many Native Americans were forced from their lands.

Some were forced into slavery. They, too, were often forbidden to speak their native languages.

Today, all U.S. citizens are guaranteed certain rights by the Constitution and the Bill of Rights. The Constitution was created and signed in the 1700s. British colonists who came to live in the United States created it. They crafted the Constitution because they wanted to be sure that they could live happily in the United States. They wanted to be treated fairly by their government. The Constitution provided a framework of national laws. It explained the basic rights of citizens. It also placed restrictions on the government.

The first ten amendments to the U.S. Constitution are called the Bill of Rights. These amendments outline certain individual rights. They also ensure that the government cannot gain too much power. By limiting the power of the government, people know that their personal rights will be protected.

Before the Constitution and Bill of Rights became the foundations for U.S. law, other, similar documents existed. Among them were the Magna Carta, the English Bill of Rights, the Virginia Declaration of Rights, and the French Declaration of the Rights of Man and of the Citizen. The U.S. Bill of Rights was based on the same ideas and principles as some of these other documents. These documents are testimony of the evolution of human rights. With the creation of each of these documents came more restrictions on the power of governments and increased rights for people.

MAGNA CARTA AND THE ENGLISH BILL OF RIGHTS

MAGNA CARTA

The history of the U.S. Bill of Rights goes back to thirteenth century England. The men who wrote the Bill of Rights were colonists who had traveled to the United States from England. They left their home country because they did not agree with the way that the government was controlling the people. They wanted more freedoms than their government allowed. They thought the only way they could live their lives the way they wanted would be to establish their own country.

Centuries before the colonists left England for the United States, the English people suffered under their king's rule. In the 1200s, the king of England had complete control over the people of his country.

King John ruled England from 1199 to 1216. Some people have said that he was the worst king England ever had. During his reign, King John led the British military in a battle against King Philip II of France. By 1204, King John had lost the battle and considerable land to the French. He also lost the support of his people.

King John

King John spent a lot of money trying to recover the lost land. He taxed the English citizens heavily to pay for these expenses. In addition to high taxes, King John collected money from the people who had not offered their military service. Such a fee is called *scutage*. This fee was excessive. King John collected 11 scutages during his 17-year reign—the same number of scutages that King Henry II and King Richard I collected in their combined reigns of 45 years.

Around the same time, King John clashed with Pope Innocent III. When John became king, he chose an archbishop that the pope did not approve of. The pope was angry. He forced King John out of the Catholic Church. In fact, he closed all Catholic churches in England. He only allowed them to be used for baptisms and the confessions of people who were dying. King John tried desperately to regain the favor of the church. He even offered England to the service of the pope. This desperate attempt to recover the church's favor did nothing for King John. It only showed his weakness.

King John's barons were angry about the poor way in which he treated British citizens. They did not like all the power he had. They rebelled against him. This rebellion led to the creation of a document called the Magna Carta. *Magna Carta* means "Great Charter" in Latin. King John was forced to sign the Magna Carta or face the barons' wrath. They had invited France's King Philip II to England to side with them against King John. The threat of losing control to the French left King John no choice. On June 15, 1215, the barons met King John in a meadow near the palace, in a place called Runnymede. There the king signed the Magna Carta.

The Magna Carta promised the people of England several things. It promised them religious freedom, fair taxation, and freedom from

British barons pressure King John to sign the Magna Carta.

being imprisoned unfairly or without a trial. It also gave them the freedom to own property. It said that no one could take or use their belongings without payment or permission. It also ordered the king to pay the people any money that had been taken from them unfairly. It ordered the government to return any belongings that had been taken from people unlawfully.

The Magna Carta also ordered that 25 barons be elected. Their job was to keep the peace and to protect the freedoms of the people. They also made sure that any complaints about the government were addressed quickly. If a person's complaint was not addressed within 40 days, the barons could press the government to address it until the government followed through.

Before the creation of the Magna Carta, kings did not have to obey the laws of the land. With so much freedom, it was easy for kings to cheat the British people. One of the most important ideas established by the Magna Carta was that no one, not even the king, had the right to ignore the law.

The people wrote this list of laws because they were tired of being treated unfairly by their government. The king was pressured into signing the Magna Carta in order to restore peace in England. Some say that King John did not take the Magna Carta seriously.
The original Magna Carta did not help the common people very much. It mostly protected the wealthy barons of England. It was, however, the first step in limiting the power of the king of England. The Magna Carta was revised several times before it became the document that it is today. It has evolved to become a sign of freedom for all British people.

A copy of the Magna Carta, signed by King John of England.
Barons' coats of arms and royal seals surround the document.

ENGLISH BILL OF RIGHTS

Even though the Magna Carta had been in place for more than 400 years, English monarchs continued to abuse their power. King James II ruled England from 1685 to 1688.

Before he became king, James II had converted from Protestantism to Roman Catholicism. England had declared Protestantism to be the country's official religion. Laws in England at that time did not allow Catholics to hold positions of power. Even though James II was Catholic, he became king because the monarchy was established through bloodlines.

During his reign, James II encouraged religious tolerance. Even though the official religion of England was Protestant, he showed preference for Catholic officials. He also allowed Catholics to carry guns. Protestants were not allowed to carry guns. The people thought this was unfair.

James II abused his power in many ways. He took money from the people by collecting more taxes than were approved by Parliament. He also charged excessive bail and levied fines against people accused of crimes. He even fined people before they had gone to trial for their crimes.

James II stopped enforcing some laws. He abolished others when he wanted to. He did this without the approval of Parliament. He began to organize an army. The people were outraged. A plan was created to replace the king. His daughter, Mary, and her husband, William of Orange, were asked to take his place. They were living in Holland at the time.

King James II

William and Mary came to England with a Dutch army. The British army decided to support William, and James II fled. The British people interpreted this to mean that he had given up the throne. William III and Mary II were crowned the king and queen of England.

At their coronation, William and Mary were asked to make an oath. It was a promise to follow the laws that had been approved by Parliament. These laws limited the privileges of the royal family. William and Mary agreed to these laws. On December 16, 1689, these laws, called the English Bill of Rights, became effective.

The English Bill of Rights placed increased limits on the power of the monarch and increased the involvement of British citizens in the creation and omission of laws. Their civil rights continued to expand. Several of the laws that make up the English Bill of Rights are the same, or nearly the same, as those found in the U.S. Bill of Rights. For example, both give citizens freedom from excessive fines or bail. And both protect citizens from cruel or unusual punishment.

When William and Mary agreed to follow the rules of the land, it was called the Glorious Revolution. It is sometimes called the Bloodless Revolution because it brought about social change without war.

Members of Parliament crown King William and Queen Mary.

ENGLISH BILL OF RIGHTS

The English Bill of Rights states the following:

- It is illegal to create new laws, to stop enforcing laws, or to ignore laws without the approval of Parliament.

- It is illegal to abolish laws without the approval of Parliament.

- It is illegal to have a group of rulers just for church causes.

- Members of the royal family may not collect money without the consent of Parliament.

- Anyone may file a complaint with the king. The person filing the complaint may not be taken to court for doing so.

- It is against the law to keep an active army in times of peace unless approved by Parliament.

- Protestants may own guns for their defense as allowed by law.

- Parliament will be elected through free elections.

- Freedom of speech and discussions in Parliament may not be questioned in court or outside of Parliament.

- Excessive bail or fines and cruel or unusual punishments are not allowed.

- People have the right to be tried in court by a group of their peers.

- No one can be fined before being brought to trial.

- Parliament should meet regularly.

VIRGINIA DECLARATION OF RIGHTS

The first British colonists landed in North America in the late 1570s and early 1580s. They were unable to make a home there. Some returned to England because the weather conditions were too harsh. One group of colonists disappeared altogether. No one knew if they died or if Native Americans had adopted them. Their colony came to be known as "the lost colony."

The British made a second attempt to inhabit North America in the early 1600s. Two groups of merchants asked the king's permission to send a group of colonists. At that time they called America "Virginia." It was given that name by a man named Sir Walter Raleigh. In 1605, King James I signed a charter giving British explorers the right to mine any gold, silver, or copper they found in America. In 1607, the first British settlement was established at Jamestown.

British colonists came to America for two main reasons. The first was economic. During the 1500s, sheep farming had become profitable in England. People who raised sheep used the wool to make cloth, which they sold throughout Europe. Landowners took

Early colonists arrive on the shores of Jamestown, Virginia.

land away from the poor farmers who rented it. They used it as pastureland for their sheep. Without land to farm, the poor became poorer and unemployment rose.

The British government came up with a solution to this problem. It decided to send the poor and unemployed people to America. In America, they could produce raw materials, such as wood, from the resources there. These raw materials could be shipped back to England. Then they would be used to make products that could be distributed in Europe.

The second reason the British came to America was for religious freedom. The Church of England was forced upon the British people.

But not everyone wanted to belong to the Church of England. Some people were Catholics. Others were Protestants who thought that the Church of England was too similar to the Catholic Church. These people were called Puritans. Both Protestants and Catholics wanted the freedom to practice their religions without prejudice. The people who went to America for religious reasons were called Pilgrims.

In America, life was still difficult. By 1774, the British parliament had sent a general to the colonies. His job was to act as governor in the Massachusetts Colony. England was still taxing colonists. British soldiers were living in colonists' homes. The colonists thought that England's king had too much control in the colonies. From September to October 1774, the first Continental Congress met. Members tried to come up with a solution to free them from British control. At the congress, the idea of declaring independence from England became more real.

In April 1775, British soldiers confronted colonial soldiers. They started to fight, and the American Revolution began. The second Continental Congress met again that May. The colonists chose George Washington to lead their army in the war against England.

The American Revolution raged. In 1776, the American colonies began their push toward independence. On June 12, 1776, Virginia adopted its own declaration of rights. It guaranteed Virginians certain rights under the law.

The Virginia Declaration of Rights was written by George Mason. He thought of himself as a private citizen, but he was active in government from 1776 to 1787. Mason had close ties to Thomas

DID YOU KNOW?

GEORGE WASHINGTON

George Washington was the first president of the United States. He served two terms. Many people wanted him to serve longer, but Washington refused. During his life, Washington was also a surveyor, a general, and a farmer.

GEORGE MASON

Even though George Mason was from the South, he opposed slavery. At the 1787 Constitutional Convention, he tried to get the delegates to abolish slavery. Mason did not win the fight to stop slavery, but he did help get the Bill of Rights put into the U.S. Constitution.

THOMAS JEFFERSON

Thomas Jefferson is most famous for writing the Declaration of Independence. But he also was the third president of the United States. During his term, Jefferson doubled the size of the United States with the Louisiana Purchase.

A scene from the American Revolution

*****

The 13 colonies won their independence from Britain in the American Revolution. The war began in April 1775 with the battles of Lexington and Concord and ended in 1783 with the Treaty of Paris. Britain was the strongest country in the world at the time and had a professional army. The colonies put together a citizen army with inexperienced officers. With France's help, the colonists were able to defeat the well-trained British forces.

Jefferson and others who later drafted and signed the U.S. Constitution. Thomas Jefferson said that Mason was "the wisest man of his generation."

The people of Virginia were pleased with the Virginia Declaration of Rights. It not only explained individuals' rights, but also put limitations on the power of the government. This was important to Virginians. They were angry that England had been forcing colonists to pay taxes without giving them any voice in their government. They felt that the British government had too much control in the colonies. They wanted a voice in their government.

Thomas Jefferson with the U.S. Constitution

Other U.S. colonies copied the Virginia Declaration of Rights. They used its ideas in their own bills of rights. Thomas Jefferson later used the ideas from the Virginia Declaration of Rights in the opening paragraphs of the Declaration of Independence.

The Virginia Declaration of Rights became the foundation for both the Declaration of Independence and the U.S. Bill of Rights. People's rights continued to evolve. They gained more rights and their role in their government expanded.

VIRGINIA
DECLARATION OF RIGHTS

The Virginia Declaration of Rights states the following:

- All men are free and independent. As people, they have the right to life, freedom, and property. They have the right to be happy and safe.
- People have the power, and government officials must work for the good of the people.
- Government is set up to benefit and protect the people. If the government is not working for the people, they have the right to change or replace it by a majority vote.
- No person, including any government official, has more privileges than another.
- The legislative and executive powers of the state should be separate from the judicial powers. Elections should be held regularly and often.
- People have the right to vote freely.
- Laws cannot be made or abolished without the consent of the people's representatives.
- People have the right to be informed of legal charges against them. They have the right to a speedy trial by jury. No one is required to present evidence against himself.
- People cannot be charged excessive bail or fines. They cannot be punished in ways that are cruel or unusual.
- A search warrant is required to search any place or take anyone into custody.
- Trial by jury is preferred in disputes between people.
- Freedom of the press is guaranteed.
- A well-regulated army is appropriate for the safety of the people, but should be avoided in times of peace.
- People have the right to one unified government. Other governments cannot be set up in the state of Virginia.
- Justice and virtue are necessary for a free government.
- Religion cannot be forced on anyone, and people are free to worship the religion of their choice. It is the duty of everyone to be caring toward one another.

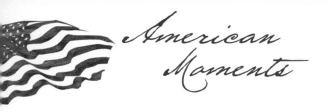

A NATION IS BORN

In 1776, Thomas Jefferson wrote the Declaration of Independence and the United States declared itself independent from England. In the Declaration of Independence, Jefferson outlined the reasons that the colonists wanted their freedom from England. He also stated the freedoms that the new United States would exercise as an independent country. Many of these freedoms reflected those included in the Virginia Declaration of Rights. Fifty-six representatives from the 13 colonies signed the Declaration of Independence.

After the United States declared its independence, each state wrote a constitution. The state constitutions outlined the rights and regulations of each state.

It wasn't until 1781 that British troops finally put down their guns and stopped fighting the colonists. Two years later, the United States and England began peace talks. Representatives from both nations met in Paris, France. They signed a peace treaty on February 3, 1783. It was at this time that England recognized the United States as an independent nation.

As time wore on, U.S. government leaders decided that it would be better for the people if the states banded together. They decided to form one unified government. They organized a Constitutional Convention in Philadelphia, Pennsylvania, to discuss a plan.

Left to right:
Benjamin Franklin, John Adams,
and Thomas Jefferson draft the
Declaration of Independence.

Representatives from the 13 colonies sign the Declaration of Independence.

Seventy-four men were chosen to represent people from all of the states. Only fifty-five of them were able to attend the meetings.

The first Constitutional Convention met on May 25, 1787. The men discussed the states' problems. They met several more times to talk about solutions to these problems. They decided to write a constitution for the whole nation. On August 6, 1787, the first draft of the Constitution was accepted. But not all members of the group liked the way the Constitution looked. They continued to meet to revise it and to talk about their ideas.

On September 17, 1787, all but three members of the Constitutional Convention accepted and signed the Constitution. It was printed and then sent to the states for signatures.

Members of the Constitutional Convention were divided into two groups. One group was the federalists. The federalists liked the Constitution as it was. The other group was the anti-federalists. Members of this group thought that the Constitution needed a bill of rights that would limit the government's power. They were afraid that without a bill of rights, the government could take advantage of the people, like the English kings had done.

Mason was an anti-federalist. He refused to sign the Constitution without a bill of rights attached to it. Two other anti-federalists also refused to sign it. They, too, wanted a promise that a bill of rights would be added.

Jefferson responded to the request for a bill of rights. He said, "A bill of rights is what the people are entitled to against every government on earth, general or particular, and what no just government should refuse or rest on inference."

In February 1788, Massachusetts signed the Constitution with the agreement that a bill of rights would be attached to it. Other states followed. The Constitution became legal on June 21, 1788.

When Virginia finally signed the Constitution, it offered a list of amendments. These were suggestions for the bill of rights. They were the same ideas included in the Virginia Declaration of Rights.

James Madison went on to become the fourth president of the United States.

A Bill of Rights

as provided in the Ten Original Amendments to

The Constitution of the United States

in force December 15, 1791.

Article I

Congress shall make no law respecting an establishment of religion, or prohibiting the free exercise thereof; or abridging the freedom of speech, or of the press; or the right of the people peaceably to assemble, and to petition the Government for a redress of grievances.

Article II

A well regulated Militia, being necessary to the security of a free State, the right of the people to keep and bear Arms, shall not be infringed.

Article III

No Soldier shall, in time of peace be quartered in any house, without the consent of the Owner, nor in time of war, but in a manner to be prescribed by law.

Article IV

The right of the people to be secure in their persons, houses, papers, and effects, against unreasonable searches and seizures, shall not be violated, and no Warrants shall issue, but upon probable cause, supported by Oath or affirmation, and particularly describing the place to be searched, and the persons or things to be seized.

Article V

No person shall be held to answer for a capital, or otherwise infamous crime, unless on a presentment or indictment of a Grand Jury, except in cases arising in the land or naval forces, or in the Militia, when in actual service in time of War or public danger; nor shall any person be subject for the same offence to be twice put in jeopardy of life or limb; nor shall be compelled in any Criminal Case to be a witness against himself, nor be deprived of life, liberty, or property, without due process of law; nor shall private property be taken for public use, without just compensation.

Article VI

In all criminal prosecutions, the accused shall enjoy the right to a speedy and public trial, by an impartial jury of the State and district wherein the crime shall have been committed, which district shall have been previously ascertained by law, and to be informed of the nature and cause of the accusation; to be confronted with the witnesses against him; to have compulsory process for obtaining Witnesses in his favor, and to have the Assistance of Counsel for his defence.

Article VII

In Suits at common law, where the value in controversy shall exceed twenty dollars, the right of trial by jury shall be preserved, and no fact tried by a jury shall be otherwise re-examined in any Court of the United States, than according to the rules of the common law.

Article VIII

Excessive bail shall not be required, nor excessive fines imposed, nor cruel and unusual punishments inflicted.

Article IX

The enumeration in the Constitution, of certain rights, shall not be construed to deny or disparage others retained by the people.

Article X

The powers not delegated to the United States by the Constitution, nor prohibited by it to the States, are reserved to the States respectively, or to the people.

Regards of Harry B. Hawes.

Soon the states elected members of Congress. During the first session of Congress, James Madison introduced a bill of rights. More than 200 amendments had been proposed by the states. Madison narrowed that number down to 24. Congress eventually agreed on 12 amendments. On September 25, 1789, these amendments were sent to the states for approval.

Within six months, 10 of the amendments were accepted by nine states. The amendments needed 11 states' approval before they would become legal. On December 15, 1791, Virginia became the eleventh state to approve the amendments. These ten amendments officially became part of the Constitution. They were called the Bill of Rights.

The people who wrote and signed the Constitution and Bill of Rights knew how important it was to define the relationship between citizens and their government. These documents guarantee U.S. citizens a voice in their government and freedom to exercise their human rights.

BILL OF RIGHTS

There are ten amendments in the Bill of Rights, but the states proposed far more. Many of the amendments the states originally proposed would have made changes to the structure of the government. Some of these amendments would have changed the powers of government.

James Madison wanted to avoid these kind of amendments. Instead, he wanted to include amendments in the Bill of Rights that would protect people's rights. The first ten amendments of the Constitution focus on individual rights. Later amendments in the Constitution deal with the structure and power of the government.

THE U.S. BILL OF RIGHTS

- **Amendment 1**–Religious freedom and freedom of speech and the press. This means that people may practice any religion they want. It also gives them the right to speak their minds and to gather peacefully.

- **Amendment 2**–The right to bear arms. This gives U.S. citizens the right to own guns.

- **Amendment 3**–The government cannot force people to house military. This means that the government cannot force homeowners to let soldiers stay in their homes.

- **Amendment 4**–Freedom from illegal searches or seizures. This means that no one may search a person or his home without a reason, or without a search warrant. No one can take another person's belongings without a warrant.

- **Amendment 5**–A person is innocent until proven guilty; no one can be forced to bear witness against him/herself. This means that no one can be punished for a crime until he/she has been proven guilty of that crime in court. It also means that no one is required to say anything in court that might prove him/her guilty of a crime.

- **Amendment 6**–The right to a speedy and public trial, and the right to a lawyer. This means that people do not have to wait a long time for a trial after they are charged with a crime. It also means that if someone cannot afford a lawyer to defend him/her in court, the court must provide a lawyer for that person.

- **Amendment 7**—Right to a trial by jury. This means that a person accused of a crime has the right to be tried in court by a group of citizens like him/herself.

- **Amendment 8**—Freedom from cruel or unusual punishment and freedom from excessive bail. This means that the courts must give people punishments that are equal to the severity of their crimes. It also means that people convicted of crimes cannot be tortured and bail cannot be unreasonably high.

- **Amendment 9**—People have other freedoms that are not listed in the Constitution or the Bill of Rights.

- **Amendment 10**—States have powers that are not granted to the federal government. This means that any powers not given to the federal government are determined by the states.

FRENCH DECLARATION OF RIGHTS

Meanwhile, in 1789 the French adopted a document called the French Declaration of the Rights of Man and of the Citizen. It was inspired by the U.S. Declaration of Independence. The French Declaration became one of the most important texts in French history.

France had been under the rule of an absolute monarchy. This meant that the king held all power. The kings who ruled France before the revolution had struggled with the costs of war losses. King Louis XIV ruled from 1643 to 1715. He lost several wars during his reign. Following was King Louis XV, and then King Louis XVI. Both of them had also spent large sums of money on costly wars. The people did not like how their kings kept spending money on wars that they did not win. French citizens were growing increasingly upset with their government. In 1789, the French began a revolution.

At the time of the French Revolution, the French people were divided into three groups, called estates. The first estate was clergy. They were representatives of the church. The second estate was nobles. They belonged to the military. The third estate was commoners.

King Louis XVI is surrounded by an angry mob during the French Revolution.

The commoners included landowners, or the upper class, and farmers, who were called peasants.

Though French citizens were divided into classes, they were united by angry feelings toward their government. The nobles were unhappy because the monarchy had taken their power away. The upper class was angry because the nobles had more privileges than they had. Both the peasants and the upper class were unhappy with France's system of taxation. Only the commoners were required to pay taxes. French peasants suffered horribly under the system. France's peasant population was growing steadily, and more peasants meant a greater demand for land. Land was divided into smaller and smaller plots so each family could have its own land to farm. The size of the plots became so small that they were barely large enough to support the needs of a peasant family.

The harvests of 1787 and 1788 were poor. Peasants were hardly able to feed their families. They had no grain or vegetables left over to sell. War debt had led to tax increases, and peasants could not pay their taxes.

At this time, people around the world were standing up for their rights. In America, settlers in Virginia wrote a declaration of rights. Other colonies were writing their own bills of rights. The French were especially influenced by the revolution in America. They were encouraged by the colonists' ideas about freedom and government. They wanted some of the same rights for themselves.

On May 5, 1789, King Louis XVI held a meeting with the Estates General, a group of people who represented all French citizens. At the meeting, the king announced that the two upper estates would

Jean-Jacques-François Le Barbier painted this depiction of the French Declaration of the Rights of Man and of the Citizen in 1789.

have to start paying taxes. The taxes were too big a burden for just the third estate to pay. The king thought that all citizens should be treated equally. This included equal representation in government. Before then, the commoners received fewer votes than clergy or nobles.

On June 17, the commoners, who made up more than 95 percent of the population, declared themselves the National Assembly. They would be the people's representatives in government. They decided that they would no longer listen to the king. They also said that they would fight until France had a constitution.

The king was startled. He had no choice but to let the people have a voice in government. He decided to allow the National Assembly to become France's parliament.

On July 14, the people attacked the Bastille. This was the state prison. It was a symbol of oppression to the French people. The uprising showed the aristocracy that the people wanted to have control of their country and their government.

On August 4, the National Assembly met. Members of the National Assembly who had privileges gave them up. All agreed to pay taxes. This marked the informal end of the class system in France. On August 26, the National Assembly met again. It issued the Declaration of the Rights of Man and of the Citizen. It declared that all people were equal. It formally abolished the class system in France.

The Declaration of the Rights of Man and of the Citizen included 17 articles. The articles outlined citizens' rights. They also restricted the power of the government. They guaranteed equality among all people.

Frenchmen attack the Bastille.

The Declaration of the Rights of Man and of the Citizen included many of the same ideas as the Magna Carta and the Virginia Declaration of Rights. Among the similarities were the human rights guaranteed to all people. They include the right to liberty, property, and equality among people. Citizens' rights expanded once they gained a voice in their government.

UNIVERSAL HUMAN RIGHTS

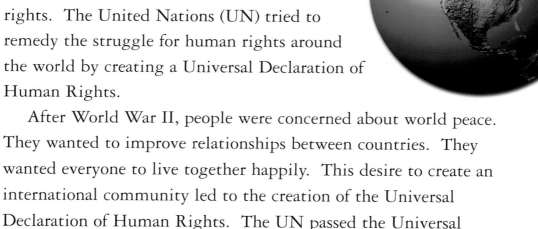

England, France, the United States, and other countries have created documents and laws that protect the rights of their citizens. But some countries have not done so. There are people around the world who still fight for basic rights. The United Nations (UN) tried to remedy the struggle for human rights around the world by creating a Universal Declaration of Human Rights.

After World War II, people were concerned about world peace. They wanted to improve relationships between countries. They wanted everyone to live together happily. This desire to create an international community led to the creation of the Universal Declaration of Human Rights. The UN passed the Universal Declaration of Human Rights on December 10, 1948. It is a symbol of the world's common goals.

The Universal Declaration of Human Rights was written by a committee of people from eight different countries. It draws on legal systems, cultures, religions, and philosophies from around the world. It is sometimes referred to as the "Magna Carta for all humanity." It has been translated into more than 200 languages.

The Universal Declaration of Human Rights outlines a broad range of rights that are considered to be free to all people. They include the right to life, freedom, and security. In addition, all people are free to earn a living, to own property, to express themselves openly, and to hold their own opinions. They have the right to education. They also have the right to be free from torture or poor treatment.

The Declaration says that the "dignity of all members of the human family is the foundation of freedom, justice and peace in the world." It is seen as the standard for all nations. It is not a legal document, but it has set a worldwide standard for human rights. The Universal Declaration of Human Rights is one of the most frequently cited human rights documents in the world. It has been used as a base for many countries' constitutions.

For centuries, people have fought against tyranny for basic human rights. Together, people and governments have worked to create human rights legislation that brings equality and freedom to all. The Magna Carta, the English Bill of Rights, the Virginia Declaration of Rights, the French Declaration of the Rights of Man and of the Citizen, and the Universal Declaration of Human Rights assure these basic rights to people all over the world. In the United States, the Bill of Rights is a guarantee of these rights for all Americans.

"ALL HUMAN BEINGS ARE BORN FREE AND EQUAL IN DIGNITY AND RIGHTS."

—Excerpt from Article 1 of the Universal Declaration of Human Rights

TIMELINE

1215 King John signs the Magna Carta.

1607 First English settlement is built at Jamestown.

1607 to 1732 First 13 colonies are established on the east coast of the United States.

1689 On December 16, the English Bill of Rights is passed.

1775 American Revolution begins.

1776 On June 12, the Virginia Declaration of Rights is adopted.

Thomas Jefferson writes the Declaration of Independence. On July 4, colonists declare the United States independent from England.

1781 The American Revolution ends.

1787 On May 25, the first Constitutional Convention meets.

1788 On June 21, the U.S. Constitution becomes legal.

1789 On July 14, French citizens attack the Bastille.

On August 26, the Declaration of the Rights of Man and of the Citizen is issued.

1791 On December 15, the Bill of Rights becomes part of the Constitution.

1948 The UN passes the Universal Declaration of Human Rights.

American Moments

FAST FACTS

England's King James II was Catholic even though Protestantism was the official religion of England when he came to power.

George Mason wrote the Virginia Declaration of Rights. James Madison drew heavily on the ideas in the Virginia Declaration when he drafted the U.S. Bill of Rights. The Virginia Declaration was also influential in the writing of France's Declaration of the Rights of Man and of the Citizen.

Before the French Revolution, only the lower class, called the third estate, paid taxes in France. The first and second estates, made up of wealthy clergy and nobles, did not pay taxes.

Two of the men who attended the Constitutional Convention later became U.S. presidents. They were George Washington and James Madison. Madison is sometimes called the "Father of the Constitution."

There are 27 amendments to the U.S. Constitution.

The Universal Declaration of Human Rights was written by UN members from eight different countries. The contributors were from Australia, Chile, China, France, Lebanon, the Soviet Union, the United Kingdom, and the United States. The outline of the document was 400 pages long! It took two years to write the final declaration.

WEB SITES
WWW.ABDOPUB.COM

Would you like to learn more about the Bill of Rights? Please visit **www.abdopub.com** to find up-to-date Web site links about the Bill of Rights and other American moments. These links are routinely monitored and updated to provide the most current information available.

Amendment I
cting an establishment of religion, or prohibiting the free exe of the people peaceably to assemble, and to petition the Gove

Amendment II
ssary to the security of a free State, the right of the people, to l

Amendment III
be quartered in any house, without the consent of the Owner,

Amendment IV
in their persons, houses, papers, and effects, against unreaso but upon probable cause, supported by Oath or affirmation, to be seized.

Amendment V
for a capital, or otherwise infamous crime, unless on a prese aval forces, or in the Militia, when in actual service in time to be twice put in jeopardy of life or limb; nor shall be d of life, liberty, or property, without due process of law

GLOSSARY

archbishop: in Christianity, the highest-ranking bishop.

charter: a written contract that states a colony's boundaries and form of government.

coronation: a ceremony to crown a head of state.

parliament: the highest lawmaking body of some governments.

Protestant: a Christian who does not belong to the Catholic Church.

Roman Catholic: a Christian whose religious group is headed by the pope.

United Nations (UN): a group of nations created in 1945. Its goals are peace, human rights, security, and social economic development.

Tourists listen to a lecture on the U.S. Constitution at the National Archives Building in Washington DC.

American Moments

INDEX